# Tia's New Neighbor

By: Jessica Horne

Illustrated by: M. Flowers

First printing, 2021

ISBN paperback: 978-1-7375494-0-6

ISBN eBook: 978-1-7375494-1-3

LCCN: 2021913723

Illustrations by:  M. Flowers

Printed in the United States of America

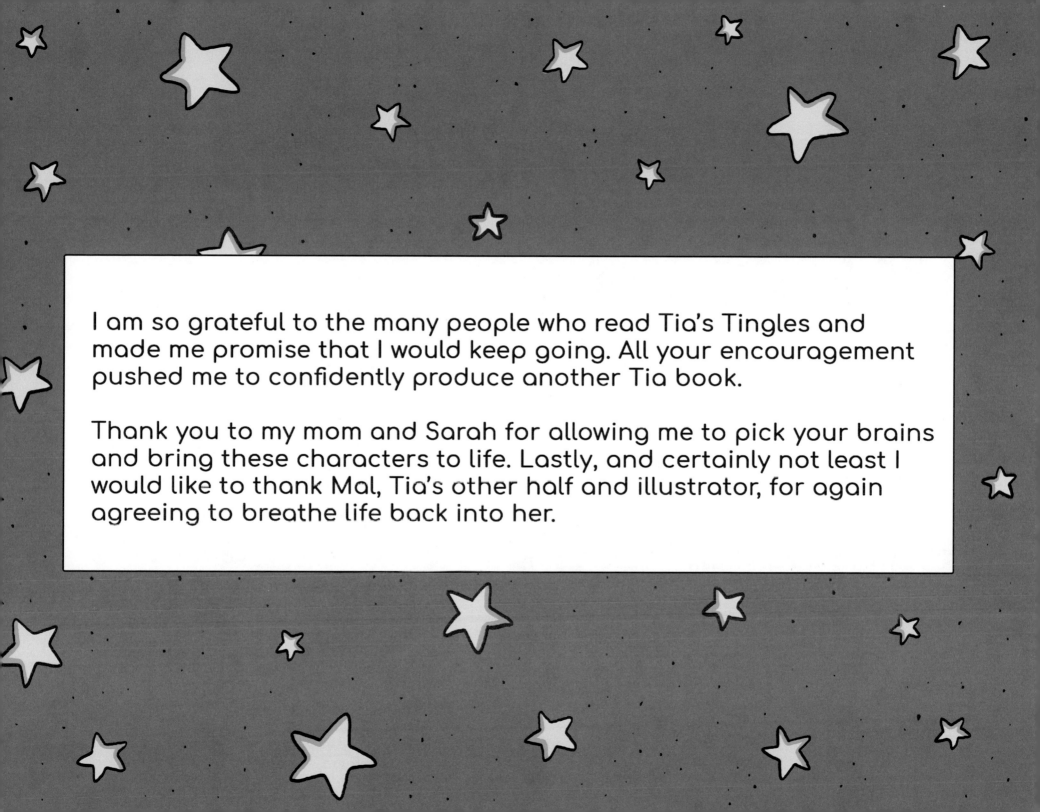

I am so grateful to the many people who read Tia's Tingles and made me promise that I would keep going. All your encouragement pushed me to confidently produce another Tia book.

Thank you to my mom and Sarah for allowing me to pick your brains and bring these characters to life. Lastly, and certainly not least I would like to thank Mal, Tia's other half and illustrator, for again agreeing to breathe life back into her.

"Yes mom?" Tia answers.
"We are meeting our new neighbors today. Maybe you can make a nice card to welcome them to the neighborhood. It doesnt have to say much just do your best", said Tia's mom.

Tia's mom hurried her along.
"Ok Tia, now let's bake some cookies!"

"Hello! My daughter and I would like to welcome you to the neighborhood. We brought you some warm cookies and a card too, right Tia?"

Excitedly Tia says, "Yep! Hi I'm Tia and who are your kids? Can they play with me and the rest of us when we play outside?"

Mr. Nawaz begins to introduce his family. "Oh hi Tia! I am Mr. Nawaz, this is my wife Mrs. Nawaz and these two are my sons Naeem and Umar. Thank you for the card and the delicious cookies."
"Nice to meet you Tia I'm Umar", replies their eldest son.

Mrs. Nawaz reaches down to her son Naeem. "Naeem, would you like to say hi to Tia and her mom?" Naeem becomes slightly agitated while hugging tighter to the ball in his hands.

"Thats alright Naeem."
"You see it can be difficult for
 Naeem to express himself around others.
 I'm sure he would like that Tia."

On the walk back home Tia looks up and asks, "Mom, do you think Naeem will come out and play with us? He didnt seem very nice. He didnt even say hi."

"Tia just give him some time. Naeem is new to the neighborhood. I'm sure he will come around to play with you and your friends in no time."

knock! knock! knock! Mrs. Nawaz answered the door surprised by the friends' visit. "Oh hi everyone! How can I help you?"
"Hi Mrs. Nawaz can Naeem come outside and play soccer with us?", asked Devy. Mrs Nawaz wanted so much for Naeem to make new friends; however she felt worried about Naeem's desire to do so. "Urrr...ummm...let me get Naeem and ask him, but before I do may I share something with you all? Naeem really enjoys playing and it will take him some time to become familiar with so many children. Be paitient with Naeem and let him come to you."

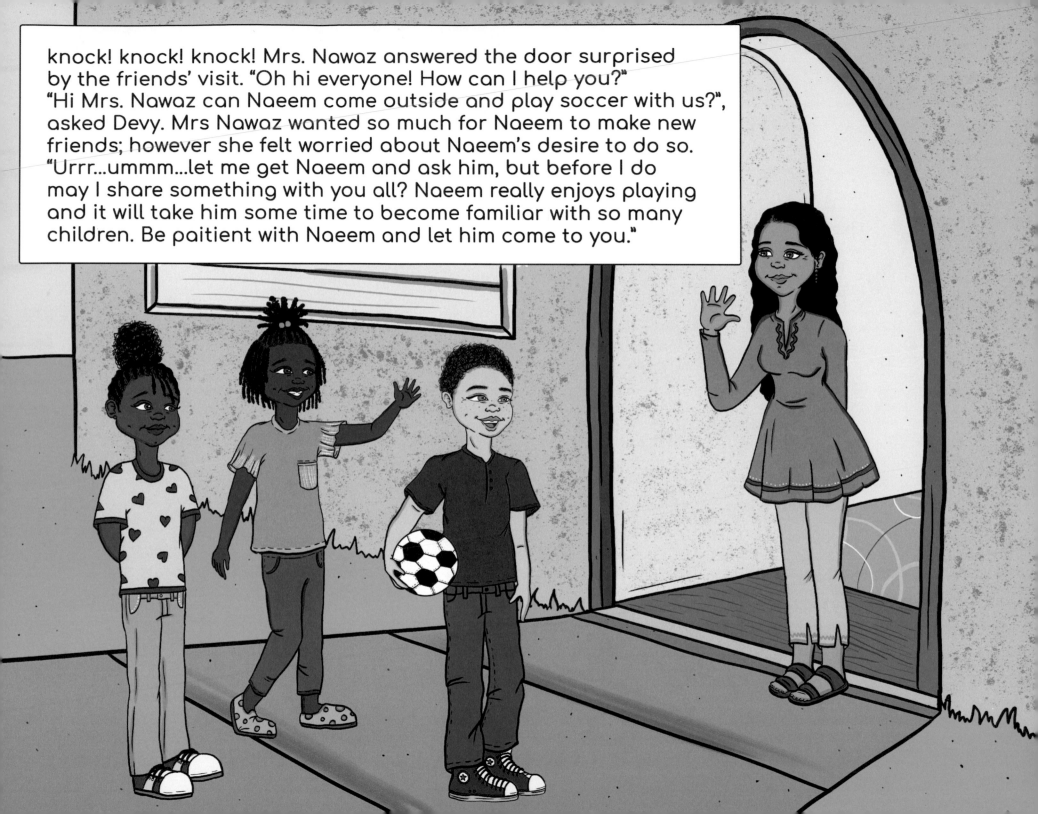

"Hey Naeem...can we play with your ball?", Cali asked. Naeem quickly becomes agitated saying no and begins to play with his ball alone.
"Well would you like to play with ours?", Devy asks.
"No!" Naeem retorts and continues to play on his own.

Mrs. Nawaz offers a gentle reminder to Tia and her friends. "Remember what I said....give it some time... why dont you begin playing and see if he will come to you?" So the friends begin kicking the ball around.

"Naeem, can you kick your ball like Tia?" says Mrs. Nawaz. "Like this Naeem..." and Tia leans back and kicks her ball over to Naeem. Instead of kicking it back Naeem walks over to Mrs. Nawaz and tugs on her leg.
"Okay Naeem, maybe next time yes?"

Everyday for the next week Tia and her friends went to check in on Naeem. They went to see if he would come outside for soccer and everyday Naeem came out to play for a little while longer but only with his own blue ball.

By Friday, Tia's mom found her on her bed and she appeared discouraged. "What's wrong Tia?"
"Cali, Devy and I have tried so hard to get Naeem to come out and play but when he comes out he just plays with his own blue ball by himself. He doesnt let any of us play with his ball either."

Tia's mom embraced her and offered her a gentle reminder, "Do you remember when Mrs. Nawaz asked you and your friends to let Naeem come to you? It seems to me she wants you to have patience and show Naeem how to play together as friends. Try not to feel down Tia and just keep trying."

On the following Monday Tia went to Naeem's door alone and asked him to kick the ball around with just her. At first Naeem put his ball on the ground and rolled it to Tia. Tia rolled the ball back to Naeem. Naeem finally kicked the ball to Tia and they began playing a game of back and forth kick ball.

That evening Tia ran into the living room where her mother and father were sitting. She told them all about the fun she and Naeem had kicking the ball back and forth. Tia had welcomed new neighbors and patiently made a new friend.

# TIA'S NEW NEIGHBOR
# ACTIVITY BOOK

## FUN ACTIVITIES TO ENGAGE YOUNG READERS

Please note that the use of each activity is dependent on the age and capability of each child.

WE ARE AMAZINGLY DIFFERENT FROM ONE ANOTHER. FOR SOME MAKING FRIENDS COMES EASY AND FOR OTHERS THE PROCESS OF BEING SOCIAL IS OVERWHELMING. BELOW DRAW A PICTURE AND RETELL THE STORY OF HOW YOU MET ONE OF YOUR CLOSEST FRIENDS.

_____

_____

_____

# QUESTIONS ABOUT THE STORY

1) When Tia first noticed a new neighbor was moving in she excitedly began thinking of all the fun things they could do together. What fun things do you like to do with your friends?

2) Tia and her mom introduced themselves to their new neighbors by writing a welcome letter and baking them cookies. What are other ways to introduce yourself to a new friend?

3) In the story Naeem was hesitant to play with Tia and her friends, how did the friend's react to this?

4) Naeem had a favorite toy that he enjoyed playing with. Do you have a favorite toy that you like to play with? Do you share your favorite toy with friends?

5) Tia used the support of her mother and friends when she needed help forming a friendship with Naeem. Who do you look to for support in times of difficulty?

# TIA'S WORD SEARCH

Neighbor
Ball
Patience
Respect
Play
Support
Meet
Friends
Trust
Fun

J P F R I E N D S Z
T X Z P M P K S H M
R N A A B L W X B E
E E A T S A N T A E
S I B I U Y W R L T
P G C E P Y F U L B
E H P N P S U S S H
C B X C O J N T U E
T O I E R F H U P R
G R O O T Q E Y L A

# Dramatic Play

Dramatic Play (costume/dress up optional):
Have the children in your classroom, group, or home find and choose dress up clothing. Ask each child to choose a name to represent who they are pretending to be. After everyone has chosen a name ask them to think of one or two special things about their person that they would like the group to know. Once each child has chosen a name, persona, and their special characteristics have them go around the room reintroducing themselves to one another.

## Discussion:

1) How did you choose to introduce your new self?

2) How did you feel introducing a new you to another person or a group of people?

3) How did you decide who would go first and who would go next in the conversation?

4) Did your new self share something in common with another person?

5) When you did not share something in common how did you keep the conversation going?

The truth is not all friendships work out. Some go their separate ways over time and some just don't develop at all. Discuss a time when a friendship didn't work out and how that made you feel.

_____

_____

_____

_____

_____

_____

# WHAT WOULD YOU DO?

For this activity you will need a pair of dice. Each participant will roll the dice and read the scenario that matches the number rolled. After reading your scenario discuss what you would say and do if placed in that situation.

1) You go to a friend's home for a playdate and their parent offers you a snack you don't like.

2) Your classmate passes out invitations to their birthday party. You don't receive an invitation.

3) Summer has come and your parent(s) chose a new summer camp for you to attend. You don't know anyone there and you've been nervous about the first day. One of the camp counselors asks if you'd like to introduce yourself to some of the campers.

4) A group of kids in your neighborhood are playing ball and you want to join in.

5) You are coloring with your friends and you need a red crayon to finish your picture.

6) You are given a gift from your parent(s) that you don't like.

7) Your parent comes home tired from work. You've been waiting for their arrival so they can help you finish putting together a difficult puzzle. Your parent lets you know that they are too tired tonight and can help you tomorrow after getting some rest.

8) During a lesson at school your teacher asks a question that you know the answer to. You raise your hand but the teacher calls on another student who also had their hand raised.

9) You are at an arcade with your family playing your favorite game. You have played the game for a while and other children are waiting to have a turn. You're asked to give someone else a chance to play by a trusted adult.

10) A new kid moves into your neighborhood. He comes over to play and asks to play with your favorite toy.

11) You and your parent(s) are all set to go on an outing. It's chilly outside and

12) ** Create your own scenario ** Ask another participant to create a scenario for you.

CPSIA information can be obtained
at www.ICGtesting.com
Printed in the USA
LVRC092318210721
693351LV00002B/3